SOUTHNESS

Books from LUNAR CHANDELIER PRESS

Southness by Vincent Katz 2016
A Picture of Everyone I Love Passes Through Me
    by Lynn Behrendt 2016
The Cheapskates by Jerome Sala 2014
Dick: A Vertical Elegy by Sam Truitt 2014
Tiny Gold Dress by John Godfrey 2013
Radio at Night by Laurie Price 2013
Earth after Earth by Toni Simon,
    with drawings by the author 2012
Deliberate Proof by Vyt Bakaitis 2010
petals, emblems by Lynn Behrendt 2010
Homework by Joe Elliot 2010

SOUTHNESS
VINCENT KATZ

LUNAR CHANDELIER PRESS

Copyright © 2016 Vincent Katz
All Rights Reserved. First Edition
Printed in the United States of America
ISBN: 978-0-9846076-8-6SI

Some of the poems in *Southness* were first published in the following journals: *Aufgabe, Bomb, Bombay Gin, The Brooklyn Rail, Conjunctions, Court Green, The East Village, Jacket, LiVE MAG, milk magazine, Shampoo, Shiny, Yellow Field*. The author thanks the editors of those journals for their support and outstanding attention to detail. In addition, the poems "A Dance for First People," "Ives Field," and "Steve and his Girl" were first published in Alex Katz's catalogue *Smile Again: Paintings of the Sixties*, Jablonka Galerie, Cologne, 2000; the poem "Vanitas" was first published in Francesco Clemente's catalogue *Terra Fragile*, Edition Bruno Bischofberger, Zürich, 2001; and the poem "Opacities" was first published in Robert Zandvliet's catalogue *The Varick Series*, Peter Blum Edition, NY, 2000.

The author would like to thank the following for assistance with this publication and for ongoing inspiration: Norma Cole, Jim Dine, John Godfrey, Charles Gute, Julie Harrison, Jack Kimball, Kimberly Lyons, Lilian Tone, Amy Trachtenberg, Anne Waldman. His deepest thanks to each of them. A special thank you to Vivien. And in memory of Prince.

Cover image by Etel Adnan, large detail of *Untitled*, 2014, oil on canvas
30 x 24 cm © Galerie Lelong
photo: Fabrice Gibert

Book and cover design: Julie Harrison
julie-harrison.com
Photo credit for bio: Vivien Bittencourt

Published by Lunar Chandelier Press
Brooklyn, New York 11201
www.lunarchandelier.com
lunarchandelier@gmail.com

LUNAR CHANDELIER PRESS

Delirious Avenues
lit
with the chandelier souls
of infusoria
   —Mina Loy

For Isaac and Oliver

Table of Contents

Lothian	1
Good Friday	3
Buchanan Unbowed	4
Quadro Tonto	5
Hôtel de Suède	6
Pasadena	7
Late Find	9
Clearing	10
Alba	11
Breads and Sweets	12
Moon	14
Dreams	15
To Life	16
Sun	17
Botanical	18
Change	19
Unbewusste Orte	21
Memory	22
Psalm	23
A Dance for First People	24
Ives Field	25
Steve and his Girl	26
Siren	27
Kid Finish	28
March	29
Twist	30
In Terms of Time	31

A Life Worth Living	32
Hungarian Green	33
Poem	34
Sunlit Portrait	36
An Earthen Sky	37
Luis	38
Vanitas	39
Verve's Room	42
Granite Curbs	43
Camden	44
Over Cleveland	45
The Moon	46
The Pond	47
Summer	48
Fecundity	49
Francis Bacon	50
Price	51
Ocher	52
Opacities	55
notes	65
bio	67

Lothian
to John Godfrey

a great rush
to confront solidity
events planned
co-exist in space
drawings' grace
a way of breathing
properly, not too
furiously injected
to others' arguments

but landscape's
imagining unreal
presence behind
tension, desire
eventually, if noticed
paths through epochal
hills, sheep where
soul cries out
as elsewhere
stones of
cathedrals
universities on
rocky coasts subside
long histories
do not face
echoes in geometric
window glass

then return
to cities

of races
mixed places one
moves to interpret
change in weather
rhythm a constant
hum of living
one knows
tempo of, is
never short

Good Friday

the eagle of right thought
lands at my feet and smiles
I can know each of them
without ever speaking
can tell this one is good
by the way she combs her hair
that one has a tragic failing
need to please, each breathes a
trembling, human avidity
and I know each without
speaking, like a farmer

Buchanan Unbowed

midway between two primaries
his bounce had begun to shrink
gag order imposed
liberalizing balkanized economies
sleeping alone, perpetuating fiefs
diluting virulence built on
spoils and patronage
Milan Panic's desires
exaggerate thin volume

I feel sorry for Bob Dole
not really sorry, as he is a man
of immense power and shallow moral basis,
but I pity him, as he seems
so ill-suited to the position
in which he now finds himself —
that of having to project an intelligible position
on a variety of topics

punching bag
father ordered him to slug 1,600
times a week as party
scold and satirist, barbs
salting routine stump, in Little
Havana, squawked, "We're going
to name that parrot Bob Dole"

Baton Rouge
balloon deflated, string
of losses, faded

Quadro Tonto

I'd like to be a better person
I know that in their eyes I'm fine
that everything has been left in order
but in my own I fail at intervals
I'm not enough there for people
I evanesce or my own desire's paramount

but I also know it is within my power
to be a better person
I need only look into their eyes
instead of longingly down streetlights
of the limb-strewn boulevard

Hôtel de Suède

large trees
cover sleep
rest avocation
under modernity's
glare, *la semaine
prochaine*, equally
iron-work
delicate floral
weighty tome
light to ear
deadpan lie
in bed, hotel
voices in rain
courtyard trees
garden lawn
has reason
afternoon
closes in

Pasadena

Schubert Impromptu
mineral water
flowers of the field
simple piano rage
on the radio again
calmed 3/4 simplicity
yesterday it was
in the car as I
drove to the hospital
today in the hotel room
looking out on
towering palms
hair waving
breeze, Vivien
sleeps, sprinklers
jet sun-drenched
lawn, cactus
undergrowth, I have
the typewriter
my essay, outside
impressive homes
and horticulture
lawns which end
precisely at cement
curbline, definition
of human restraint
and ambition
courtesy extended
in daily dealings
I have no desire

to battle traffic
to L.A., Pasadena
a fine world on
a hill, Saturday
we went to the desert
heat emptied
the rocks, transfigured
by mind

Late Find

grasses snake
near door
ocher stem
dance
head arms
out cold
highway air
nest
treasons flit
two deer
face
poetry barren
extend shy
logged slat
hindrance
prime
on
periphery late
in path
grey swelling
deer's insides
out
extracted

Clearing

Metropolitan hour melody
distances clear to eye
sunlit prerogatives building
plane air between circular
route down one avenue up
another stand in street
vendors stalled djellaba
zone between point
monument governor seat
blessed toy monopoly gilded
hour faces lightness drums

Alba

cloud passing in window
thicket of mushroom-top chimneys
from single root
I will cease silent assault
desist from borrowed lingo
I may not avoid
sexual self-harassment
but I will try
                   a drink, an ale
in cavern of artistic vegetation
alba lights my night to self
revelation, collapse, tinker
sentiments in cold
police car blue

Breads and Sweets

bridling with unseen
energy, listen to moans
falsifications even
friends, haircut, architecture
slide downhill where everything
meshes, better than others
I lift my eyes to sink
vocal push into physical
size, body contacted
jealous of her producers
interviewers who miss
her point completely, sorry
but the songs ascend ignorance
shyly flirting segments
imagination, flaunted
intelligence, they leave her
undented in morning
actually it is I who
misunderstand from my
non-perspective, cascades
of words, piano and voice
are the weapons of armies
bolted to past thoughts and
present perceptions, refrain
the delicate intensity forked
spread up the photographs'
frankness, I want to use her
name, but not yet, the sky
has descended, earlier
we crossed the aqueduct

I live only in my life now
the words come from the
latin and they have been
preserved, I start to write
the unexpected streams
forth, didn't know I was
thinking, was I? in
galleries, streets, passing
people borne down
by disharmony
they want that watch
and thatch but greed
hovers, oh no, here
comes the satellite
descending, descending
heedless of desire
trees' grandeur in shady
boulevards, the song's
pure chant hits, evens
promised longing till
self re-emerges, washed
and inimitable, once
again able to attend
I had hoped for so much
expectation of necessity
I am outside now
September's clear
voice, indication
that shutters will
fall and open drily

Moon

reflection of sliver
wet tile
pushes trees
reed-like whistle
cotton-candy cloud
sun-filled
over ocean
baby palms overarch
fronds of spine
harmony
central note, pin
dot high in century
blue, midge insolence
baby, man
vistas into
one present
pleasant
central enhance

Dreams

dreams
dark bungalow
roar
silence
dreams life
flitting
calm portal
patio
flickers sand
leaves, day
snake
logic, body
see sky
bottom deep
vision
descend
inside, resurge

To Life
to Lúcia Lima

Ides gone unnoticed
highrise fit over park
light late faces each
a world sympathetic
                      a month
gone fresh on Forsyth, another
Ides, April to sky, filtered
sonogram, one stroke
completes its magic

light, peace, world
split open, relieved
of choices, dense bliss
connect the universe

Sun

Now I am calm
no music can ascend
glass wash in wisdom
align jarry blend.

Men in uniform bend,
honor pledge's fall.
Creases wrinkle smiles
ordained suits pardon.

Woe betide that nearby one
twinkles with a leering gun.
Suppository blanks inside a mind
breakfast for the hanging sun.

Botanical

The grass
is beautiful.
So is
the ass.

In the
park, people
join, then
separate.

Flowers
grow, lean
in sun.
You leave.

Change

There are
solutions.
Might a
turning

away not
be better,
a looking
at easier

ends? In
the city,
man bends,
woman

sighs.
Lifting
a weight,
then

a next,
library
gongs
Sunday,

spent
delicious
flow,
humanity,

body
of words.
A baby
changes

the world,
pressures
slighter,
fresher

sky. Lie
on your
back, watch
them disappear.

Unbewusste Orte

One likes to dance,
another needs to
tighten her wheel.
Every moment
is innocence.

They carry those little
packages behind them.

Shit is earth.

What motivated
"Machine Gun" Kelly?
Certainly not poetry
in that battered past.

Wisps of notes.
A wisp of a girl.

Memory

Soon, she'll go.
He'll go, they'll.
Then life will be

just the way you
want it: still,
rested, according

to schedule and
plan. But it will
be duller then,

all the laughter
and confusion,
memory, pale.

Psalm

I.
I don't regret anything,
tonight. The rain
purifies my soul.

II.
Today is a fresh day.
I have no sins.

III.
What could you have asked?
An answer quick as love.

A Dance for First People

a sagging weight
resigned strength
forfends

hodgepodge elegance
mired sanity
rust

instinctive grace
a needless rush
flustered

off the mark
sitting punching
a cold lying down

in death
in flag of country's
death

black not black
back of space
regret

yellow green
purple red
wait

hungry entity
priest vision
wrist

Ives Field

ball game on a hill
the cluttered masses
have clustered away

from city's errant freak
hard earth gradual
flower fleck in fold

child man adult wrinkle
blueberries in a peanut
butter bucket tilled

impressive hold
rest attired symbol
pressed remit intern

soft salient sky preside
over me over my
arms enfold boot

caps and light red
greens delicious
sight marble cloud

Steve and his Girl

police lease fleece
robbers drown gown

walnut sky prevented
mountain wall invert

isolate poplar wingnut
trumpet along path

dirt stone pebble hush
streams of paint rush

shore of hair skins
cranium moving

forward eyes alight
pale blue white

cool shudder at lip
black is back stroke

sculptural quest
parsing pull at rest

Siren

calm winter descending
clear day's outlook pond
sky cream shades
light sounds roof puddles
hums as in others'
towns vibrating peace
inklings rest wet
utmost grace day dies
sigh last care release
other saves beyond

Kid Finish

Something harsh,
metallic, about it,
something round
and full, winter day.

Still color in sky,
palest purple, through
which planes pass, clouds
align, snow collected

in spots, become ice,
wind blast bumps window,
siren barely audible,
lights of lives and music.

March

March grabs you by the hair
something coming from sky
clippers and calipers odd alleys
poetry come billowing up

whose sidewalks are wide enough
for kisses lingering coddles smiles
tumult of earth breaking through
park's heart cafe-hopping hackers

greeting tight jeans transformation
new young ones to make own
piles of kisses in mail egregious
mark sly mention eyeglass sex

spring raw fish jibe spew rancid
restaurant sinkhole jab unknown
wing frost moister roof allure
portion singled fret untied preen

leave in flurry of stir
onslaught demand pertinence
blue socks black shoes redress
month ebbing latent flux

Twist

dodged assimilate
attire attach.

watched whistle
work remnant.

style research
assist penury.

rest increment
retire spent.

awry reason
reckon alit.

In Terms of Time

I have to go
home

and figure
out tomorrow

some don't
have homes

in June rain
could it be worse?

lights begin
to glisten

listen within
friends with pain(t)

without sing

A Life Worth Living

I never had a chance to read that book: am I dead?
Can the dead remember the dead?
Sun beats down on the paper
The sweater, the jacket, shadows cross the road
Days that change their weather, like clothes
How do you define that blue, seen through trees?
The dog is your loyal companion on the sunny
        shadow-crossed road
Those are good honest bugs
We have to live down the other side now
Your tea was beginning to suffer the opposite of meltdown
I guess you fit under romance
Then we all got in bed and watched a basketball game
That seems a fair price he's got my car key
Dormant fields peppered by geese

Hungarian Green
for Morgan

awnless bromegrass
assets by descent
barbed processes
axminster tufts
azimuth gas gland
hellish gammadion
pied-bill grebe
hellenist hello
heraclitean
imparadise

Poem

I.

If I were swimming in a pond
Language of my generation

Walk started fresh but
Ended clammy

Can't think of a way
To change this

But you could register
Your state

To get out of myself

Come back later
Tomorrow maybe

To see it
Changed

II.

But with sons
I can't flee

The sun
So dead

Lovely it
Set on asphalt

What the walk
Could not

It seems
The poem

Achieves:
Lightness

In the window
Writing

Dusk's breeze
Across

One's ankles
And knees

Sunlit Portrait

beautiful face
the delicate look
from a tapered top lip
and fuller lower

her dog has died
"you could almost
not notice him, but
the silence, now,

is deafening"
how'd she grow
up in Little Rock?
so refined, her

look of America
but quieter
holds a photo
of Rusty now

they're all photos
light becomes
gripping, dull
and we return

to the mischievous
energy of plants
and parks and
Foosball games

An Earthen Sky

tumult upswept
wind from below
a tumulus spear

tranquil theft
a modern living
peace broker

wind from creek
populist brief
cryer political

sent days vista'd
weft astream
dropsy seals

anchor glide
abhor time-set
rebuttal

Luis

nose to grindstone
eats allowed steps
frights bathing sop
redound limit

cry by door
sun twinkle grass
now eating
crunch delight

sundown feed
shiver, pressed
onus, relax in covers'
glow sensitized

Vanitas

Quiet Zone…

I. Beauty

three flesh-toned columns
arise at our front
down urban canyon

licked a pinkish hue
half proud in dark
no more time for thought

we set out, two children
read on marble steps
she unveils herself

II. Seaside

cold as ice on set-out
lines of lights above
a pigeon huddled by

the marble, dying
the horns and whirs
of machinery readying

we push along the course
anxious steady on
full involvement

III. Roadside

a packing out
stove armories
links as mordant

a storied assault
chairs and whiskers
drunk singing

incomprehension
a wet rope flung upward
landing flat on a chest

IV. Gore

total rout, we're set
running, turmoil
the dire sense of it

nothing for mother
no seed left alongside
children, others

the road quickening
for some, blighted
persistence, wedge

V. Peace

back, we're singing
fêted though sour
girls and dances

in the library see one
another, quiet zone
silence breath

fork in the path but you
could come back always
could see one again

Verve's Room

That violence was all a part of it
It's okay about the milk

I love the workers
The ones who really get it done

Films in the gutter, the pan
Obstacles acceded friend

Blanketed lust extended
Foreign entities tiled

Granite Curbs

A paper edit.
Sliding to a halt.
Sibilant murmurs,
threatened peace.

A grinding.
Pressed minutes.

You shudder,
singly.

Shingles huddle,
plain turnip.

                Prize,
                simple eternal
                puddle
                prize champion
                priest
                whiffle
        silk tie
a ravaged purse uplift decide
prism Atta brink prism

Camden

    to the park
                down
    to the fitted granite
                      wall
    the stream empties
        out in falls

    by the dinghies

Over Cleveland

Look at those mountains
Things come out wrong

Broad, untroubled land
Below itself spread

Far as eye can see
Flat peace given

By lights, deep band
Orange thick sunset

All that order, calm
At a price arranged

The Moon

Suddenly, its visage appeared
Towering over us, yellow
In the mists, moon
Bright because of the sun

Follows us in the air, rises,
Howls yellowly, our son
Asks and tells how it shines
In the darkness it rises until

Shrouded no more but
Accrues in blackness
A terrible force, pulls
Us alone through longing

The Pond

Art's endless fascination,
as children's cartoon, seen
over and over, makes
ever better sense.

You can look at it all day,
it does not shrink, become
less delicious, fact
of temperature's time.

At the end, a wind
in the poplars, and it
is time. We can
make no other.

Summer
in memory of Mike Mazur

I don't know if he sailed or played ball
But I imagine he could have or did
He had that agility of conversation
His eyes were full of light

I could tell when we spoke
There was interest in his voice
The challenge of an idea
We could find together

He spoke like a true New Yorker
Though he lived all the time I knew him
In Massachusetts, the city and beach
In some way, I was always aware

Of his presence, through friends
Or more directly, his work
Which I'd come upon in museums
Or galleries, it always had

That surprise of discovery
It was something undefined
A beating, as of waves, toward
An undisturbed shore of friendship

Fecundity
to Alessandro Twombly

I accept anything my children give me
Those things are kept in a special place

The place of my own things has less and less importance
If I travel to another place, it is not because of me

This is something I am learning, over and over
Eventually, a calm overtakes the situation

There is waiting, and the move from place to place
But there is the non-moving too, the non-waiting

We are fathers, sons, and we share a sense of life
As something given, something received, in every moment

For example, the sun rises and causes tomatoes to ripen
The sun and the tomatoes are parts of our lives

There is no escaping the earth, or
The patterns we make on it

Those are the givens, and inevitable decay,
Weakness, are parts of it, not to be shunned

One day, the light will grow very weak,
Not the final day, but one near it

And you will realize that light too is the same
And so is its disappearance

Francis Bacon

1 *Animal*
An ache of blue in the clouds

2 *Zone*
The tension of bodies

3 *Apprehension*
A little man down the road

4 *Crucifixion*
A drink or two at the pub

5 *Crisis*
If violence be the rule, I be the exception

6 *Archive*
Photocopy is the only reality

7 *Portrait*
You look only as you look

8 *Memorial*
All that is left is sadness

9 *Epic*
All that is sadness and exultation

10 *Late*
I wish I lived here but I do live here

Price

I paid a price, but
did not learn the lesson:
time's elastic, not
measured in hours or years.

It does not matter when
or where I wrote this.
I've been keeping track
of things that do not matter.

I could not get the point.
Is there still a chance?
To add to pretty chatter
would be a harsh reward.

Ocher

A season of dishes, falls,
an optimum thrusting,
brainwaves internal fixed
steam from a window,
drinks at noon, whiskey,
but fallow, studio visit

       Regardless of the plummet, sales pitch foreground,
       summit interloped, preview canceled, the forest green
       camper, permit vista purloined jumper, previous grin

A seasoning, dipped concrete
Fiestaware, hybrid, a magic concealed
at week's, forest drippings, insight
tall magnums inserted light diminish

Concern for falling, corners tipped into light, the exhibition
one and the same, a farmer's tight-lipped consternation,
once again, a chip risen to take its place among the stands
of olives, oleander, mistaken

       and again, slipping, a time lapse
       frosted early intimate sequins
       antennae twitching at an adult camp

the former waste unit, brimming
       as such to
breach the shyster locked here

Annette touched her hat as signal
              the lock-to
warrants seasonal bypass

freezone martin symbolize

a symptom, a waning, precipice
where one could drive, feet
winning and the fact of drink

even if winter's win struck low
certain residues prefigure gloss
a system of riggings close to nests
psoriasis regal sublet fantasy

              looking into holes, climbing
              up inclines
              jog into pits, speaking into
              giant phone

              guns and fantasy

              the wits get pushed farther along
              the fathers of our country are mothers
              twigs balance the act of caring

witness where one has fallen, falls,
and one can do nothing, can see,
only look and learn, the restaurant,
all the places, the destruction,

        and fathers are their own mothers
        and we are witness to that
        and others, forgetting what we learned,
        where we were to come from,

        come upon, pushed, into focus,
        a way of losing, of continuing,
        that is music, a sound of words
        echoing in a vast piazza

season of dints, marbling
long sky pushed rivulets, quarries
salmon inside of lips, margin
achieved, a long way ago

        shards imitate delight
        weakness kneels to it
        and strength is right here too
        now, go and take a breath, a step
        down corridors of blank rays

a stifled breath
hardness, harm

Opacities

of early morning
pinions thrusting
at odd ends
a sorrowful must
minute's return
to be figured
flung a dense
resource nodded
at prodded
for once a given
solid fold
research wile
beset aloof
kindled in

astride the
Jolly Roger
roads' inway
collapsible
snow insert
breast feeling
crested align
jib up saloon
rim of sky
pack oak

norwesting
assails
senses
adrift
pinned on
nervous hoax
deprived
no guarantee
icy humps
siphon
into
pocket

circle round
notaress
release fly
plash plunging
adept circuit
willowing crest
husk register
at one flow
berated
simply offend
pressed detail
unhazarded
plush simile
unilaminar
nose-flute

the song attends, willing
ones witness whistling push
absorb the one, afloat in
morning light, seashell
hitting one's head in sun
priest berobed in light
attend rock ceremony left
beride sister's overflowing
set, she places hands toward
sunrise will-o'-the-wisp
atone merrily in soft wrest

ludic lift tend to huge snake
devil bashing head at car
window head size of side
table body large trunk of tree
thrusting questing abid
climb down to track climb
up again desire of dogs to
lie together permanently

nuzzled
frond
friend
forfend
wicked
end
simulate
pretend
origin

is lighted up
is fantasy
frisked forward
treetop indigenous
workplace sanctified
pabulum
parked
invested
torque

illicit rage purging crust
tamed to rancor on intelligence
bounced past reason no foot
to pull true lives from tops
no illness fated cresting cities'
failed obeisance truss to guilt
solitude increased as many's
one past torrid despair regain
greens browns tending rest
yellows pale rain crash scent
impinged the cuts power
control each own choices
black mood crushed destroy
no possibility saved in white

Notes

"Quadro Tonto" was written after seeing Enzo Cucchi's aquatint *Testa Tonta* at the Hamburger Bahnhof Museum in Berlin on February 5, 1997

"Vanitas" was written for the catalogue to Francesco Clemente's exhibition "Terra Fragile" at Gallery Bruno Bischofberger in Zürich in 2001

"Francis Bacon" was written after seeing the Bacon exhibition at Tate Britain in London in 2008

"Opacities" was written for the catalogue to the Robert Zandvliet exhibition "The Varick Series" at Peter Blum Gallery in New York in 2000

Other poetry books by Vincent Katz

Rooms (Open Window Books, 1978)
A Tremor in the Morning (Peter Blum Edition, 1986)
Cabal of Zealots (Hanuman Books, 1988)
New York Hello! (Ommation Press, 1990)
Boulevard Transportation (Tibor de Nagy Editions, 1997)
Pearl (powerHouse Books, 1998)
Understanding Objects (Hard Press, 2000)
Rapid Departures (Ateliê Editorial, 2005)
Judge (Edizioni Charta/Libellum Books, 2007)
Alcuni Telefonini (Granary Books, 2008)
Berlin (Saal-Presse, 2008)
One-Liners (Faux Press, 2014)
Swimming Home (Nightboat Books, 2015)

Vincent Katz is a poet, translator, critic, and curator. The author of *Swimming Home* (Nightboat Books, 2015) and *The Complete Elegies of Sextus Propertius* (Princeton University Press, 2004), he is also the editor of *Black Mountain College: Experiment in Art* (MIT Press, 2002; reprinted 2013), and he is the curator of the "Readings in Contemporary Poetry" series at Dia Chelsea. Vincent Katz lives in New York City and teaches at the Yale School of Art. Raphael Rubinstein has characterized Katz as "A 21st-century flâneur whose wanderings range from the sidewalks and subways of New York City to the crowded beaches of Rio de Janeiro."

CPSIA information can be obtained
at www.ICGtesting.com
Printed in the USA
FFOW05n0327220616